CONTENTS

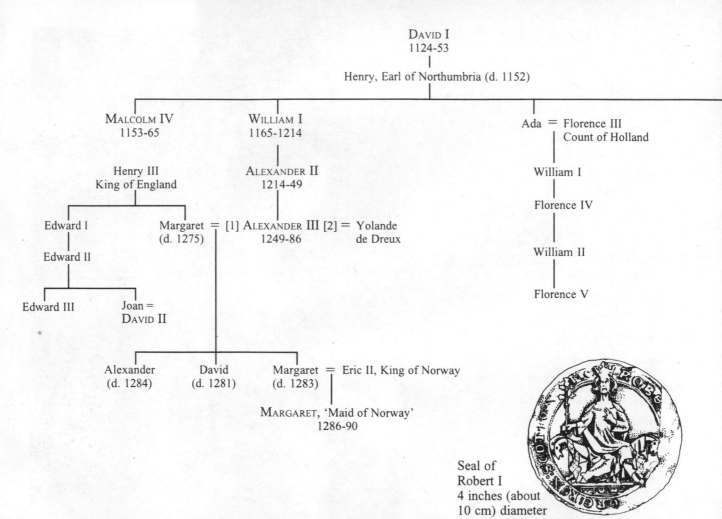

DAVID I
1124-53

Henry, Earl of Northumbria (d. 1152)

MALCOLM IV
1153-65

WILLIAM I
1165-1214

Ada = Florence III
Count of Holland

Henry III
King of England

ALEXANDER II
1214-49

William I

Florence IV

Edward I

Margaret = [1] ALEXANDER III [2] = Yolande
(d. 1275)   1249-86   de Dreux

William II

Edward II

Florence V

Edward III

Joan =
DAVID II

Alexander
(d. 1284)

David
(d. 1281)

Margaret = Eric II, King of Norway
(d. 1283)

MARGARET, 'Maid of Norway'
1286-90

Seal of
Robert I
4 inches (about
10 cm) diameter

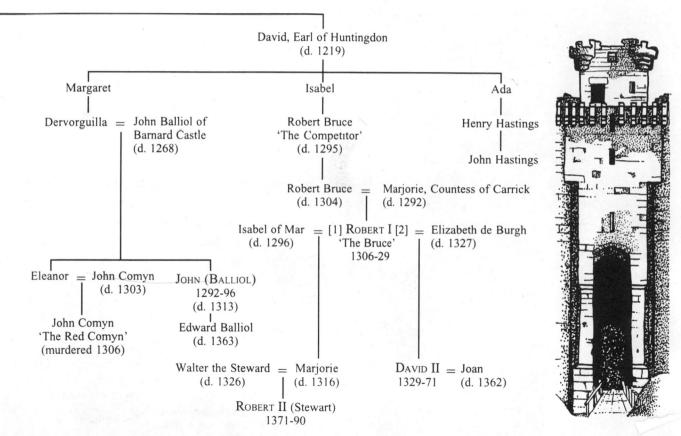

David, Earl of Huntingdon
(d. 1219)

Margaret — Isabel — Ada

Dervorguilla = John Balliol of
Barnard Castle
(d. 1268)

Robert Bruce
'The Competitor'
(d. 1295)

Henry Hastings

John Hastings

Robert Bruce = Marjorie, Countess of Carrick
(d. 1304)   (d. 1292)

Isabel of Mar = [1] ROBERT I [2] = Elizabeth de Burgh
(d. 1296)   'The Bruce'   (d. 1327)
                  1306-29

Eleanor = John Comyn   JOHN (BALLIOL)
            (d. 1303)   1292-96
                             (d. 1313)

John Comyn
'The Red Comyn'
(murdered 1306)

Edward Balliol
(d. 1363)

Walter the Steward = Marjorie
(d. 1326)   (d. 1316)

DAVID II = Joan
1329-71   (d. 1362)

ROBERT II (Stewart)
1371-90

5

The Golden Age of Alexander III

Alexander III succeeded his father as King of Scotland when he was seven years old. He reigned for 36 years. There was peace with England, because his wife, Queen Margaret, was a daughter of the English King, Henry III. There was peace at last with the dangerous Norsemen, when Alexander's daughter married the King of Norway.

Though it was a time of prosperity for many, to Alexander it brought unhappiness. His wife died in 1275, and then his two sons. There was now no male heir to succeed him. His daughter Margaret died after giving birth to a girl, also called Margaret. In 1285, hoping for a son,

During the 13th century many townships, called burghs, were founded as centres for trade. Weekly markets were held in the open space around the mercat cross. Merchants called at the tolbooth to pay taxes on their goods. The inhabitants of a burgh, the burgesses, paid rent to the King and elected their own officials.

Alexander married the young Yolande de Dreux, daughter of a French count.

That year a rumour spread that the Day of Judgement was near, when the end of the world would come. One terrible night of storm, Alexander was at Edinburgh Castle, drinking with his lords after a council meeting. Suddenly he announced that he was going to ride home to the royal manor at Kinghorn, where Yolande was, 32 kilometres (20 miles) away on the other side of the Firth of Forth.

In dreadful weather, he crossed the Forth by the ferry to the burgh of Inverkeithing. In spite of the warnings of one of the leading burgesses, who met him when he landed and offered him hospitality for the night, the King insisted on continuing his journey, and rode off ahead of his guides into the night. The next day his body was found on the shore beneath a cliff. His only surviving heir was his tiny granddaughter Margaret, the 'Maid of Norway'. The Day of Judgement had indeed arrived, for Alexander's death began the events which led to the War of Independence.

THE GUARDIANS
OF SCOTLAND

After the funeral of Alexander III, the leading men of Scotland met and appointed six 'Guardians of the Peace' (two earls, two bishops, and two barons) to govern the country on behalf of their child-queen, Margaret.

When Margaret was six years old, the Guardians agreed to a proposal by Edward I, King of England, that she should marry his infant son, Edward of Caernarvon. Edward I was the brother-in-law of Alexander III and the great-uncle of Margaret, 'Maid of Norway'. He was so keen to have Margaret in his power that he despatched a ship to Norway, filled with gifts and delicacies of food, to fetch her for the wedding. Her father, the King of Norway, sent it back without her. He wanted her to arrive in a Norwegian ship. Sadly, she died at Orkney during the voyage.

There was now no rightful ruler of Scotland. Fourteen men applied for the post of King. Four of them had a claim by birth, as descendants of

David I. They were John Balliol; the aged Robert Bruce, Lord of Annandale (known as 'The Competitor'); John Hastings (who was a Welshman); and Florence V, Count of Holland.

In perplexity, the Guardians consulted Edward I. He set up a legal court, on Scottish soil, to consider the matter. When finally the court could not agree, it asked Edward to decide. He chose John Balliol, who in law had the strongest claim. It was a bad choice for Scotland, but a good one for Edward!

The court which met to decide who should succeed to the Scottish throne consisted of 104 members: 24 nominated by Edward I, and 40 each by Balliol and Bruce, with Edward as chairman. For 18 months, with a few rest periods while ancient documents were searched for, they listened to lawyers arguing the claims of the candidates, and deliberated among themselves.

'HAMMER OF THE SCOTS'

The first thing that John Balliol did after being crowned King was to swear homage to Edward I as his overlord. The Scottish parliament was outraged. Its members appointed new Guardians (12 this time) to make decisions in the name of the King.

In 1294 Edward declared war on France and demanded that the Scottish King, with ten of his earls and 16 barons, should join his army. This was too much even for John Balliol, who made excuses. The Guardians' response to Edward was to sign a treaty with France. This meant that the Scots were now at war with the English, and in 1296 the War of Independence properly began.

While John Balliol dithered and the Guardians tried to organise their defences, Edward's army marched north from Newcastle and besieged Berwick. Seven Scottish earls crossed the border into Cumberland with a force of infantry. They burned villages, slaughtered men, stole cattle, and made an unsuccessful attack on Carlisle. Edward sacked Berwick with unbelievable cruelty and bloodshed. The Scottish earls now made another expedition, into Northumberland. They destroyed churches and monasteries as well as villages, and, it is said, burned alive two hundred schoolboys at Corbridge.

Edward's army went on to Dunbar, whose defenders sent an anguished message of help to John Balliol. A Scottish army, sent to relieve the castle, charged to defeat against the disciplined English force. That was the end of Scottish resistance for some time.

When the Scots defending Dunbar Castle saw the Scottish army approaching over the horizon, they jumped up and down, waved banners, and shouted insults at the besiegers below: 'Come and have your tails cut off, you English dogs!' (It was commonly believed in Scotland that all Englishmen had tails.)

'TOOM TABARD'

Between April and August 1296, Edward I toured eastern and central Scotland, from Berwick to Elgin and back. It was a triumphal march rather than a military campaign. Edinburgh Castle surrendered after only a week. As Edward's army approached Stirling, the defenders abandoned the castle, leaving the keys to be handed over by the janitor.

John Balliol was forced to confess that he had rebelled against his English overlord, and to give up his kingdom. His final humiliation was at Montrose, where the royal coat-of-arms was torn from his tabard (ceremonial coat): from this he got the nickname 'Toom Tabard', meaning 'Empty Coat'. Then he was taken prisoner and sent into England.

On his way north Edward had stopped at Perth, where he helped himself to the Stone of Destiny, on which for 450 years Kings of Scotland had sat to be crowned at their coronation at Scone. (There is a legend that originally it was stolen from the Irish!) Edward had the stone put in Westminster Abbey under the seat of a specially constructed coronation throne. It remained there for seven hundred years, except for a short time when in 1950 four Scottish students removed it and hid it in Scotland. Every King or Queen of England since Edward I has been crowned upon it. It was finally returned to Scotland in 1996.

Having also ordered the royal treasure and many holy Scottish relics to be sent to London, Edward called a parliament in Berwick on 28 August. Here, leading Scots who had not already done so, recorded their oath of loyalty to Edward I as ruler of Scotland. They did this by adding their names to the 'Ragman Roll', so called because of the ragged appearance of its bottom part, to which many seals were attached. Among the names missing from the list were those of Malcolm Wallace of Elderslie, in Renfrewshire, and his younger brother, William…

13

WILLIAM WALLACE

Wallace means 'Welshman', and William's ancestor, Richard Wallace, came to Scotland in about 1170. He served Walter Fitzalan, the first hereditary High Steward (or Stewart) of Scotland, and was granted lands in Kyle. William Wallace was born in Elderslie in about 1274. No one knows the exact year, or anything for certain about his childhood and youth. We do know that in May 1297 he killed William Heselrig, an unpopular Englishman who was Sheriff of Lanark.

According to one story, Wallace had a wealthy girlfriend in Lanark, called Marion Braidfute. He used to visit her secretly after he had been involved in some trouble. One night he was spotted by some English soldiers, who pursued him to Marion's house. She let Wallace out of the back door and refused to allow the soldiers to enter until he had got away. Heselrig was so angry that he either murdered Marion himself or had her murdered, and then burned her house to the ground.

Whatever the reason for it, Wallace's killing of Heselrig was the signal for Scots to rebel against the English, and to regard Wallace as their leader.

Many of the legends and stories of William Wallace first appear in a long poem describing his deeds and adventures. It was composed about 170 years after Wallace's death by Harry the Minstrel, also known as Blind Harry, who lived during the reigns of James III and James IV. Poets at the time of Harry read or recited their works at court or in a castle hall, probably to the accompaniment of a harp or other stringed instrument.

THE REVENGE OF WALLACE

For his act of violence at Lanark, Wallace was made an outlaw. He was hunted by the English, but instead of going into hiding he went out after them. His first exploit was against an English judge at Scone, 130 kilometres (80 miles) from Lanark. He and his troop of armed men rode there on horses which were probably provided by Sir William Douglas. Douglas was the Governor of Berwick when it was sacked by Edward I. Like Wallace, he wanted revenge. The judge managed to escape just before Wallace and Douglas arrived, but he left behind valuable treasure, which the Scots took.

When the people of Scotland heard about the raid on Scone, they started rebellions. The English lords retreated into their castles, from

There was so much hatred between the English and the Scots that Edward I ordered that all land in England belonging to Scots should be seized, and all Scots who were found in England should be arrested as dangerous. One of those arrested was a son of William Douglas. He was only one year old!

which it was difficult to dislodge them. The Scots got furious, and took revenge on innocent English people, even priests and women.

It was now the beginning of July 1297. Wallace was ranging the central and southern countryside of Scotland with his growing band of followers. While he was away, an English army came up against a Scottish force at Irvine. The Scots surrendered without a fight, but cleverly prolonged the talking to give Wallace time to raise a bigger army.

There are many stories about what Wallace was doing during July. Blind Harry tells us that he stormed the sea-girt fortress of Dunnottar Castle, by Stonehaven, and burned its defenders to death in the chapel; that he then marched to Aberdeen, where he destroyed a hundred English ships. If you look at the map on pages 32–33, you will see that the distance makes this improbable.

That Wallace was at the Battle of Bell o' the Brae in Glasgow is more likely. The Bishop of Glasgow had been captured by the English. His castle, which was where the Royal Infirmary is now, was occupied by the Bishop of Durham and a thousand English knights. Wallace, with three

18

hundred men, rode to Glasgow from Ayr by night. At the bridge over the river Clyde he split his force in two. Half, under his uncle, went silently by a roundabout route to a position to the south east of the castle.

Wallace marched the rest of his men noisily up the High Street towards the castle. When the English saw them coming, they charged out of the castle to do battle. The two sides met at Bell o' the Brae, where today High Street joins George Street. The place was very narrow, so there was no advantage to the English. When the battle was at its height, Wallace's uncle emerged with his men from a side street behind the English, and smashed them from the rear.

Towards the end of July, Wallace made his headquarters in Selkirk Forest. More and more Scots joined him. The chief of these was Andrew Murray, who brought his own infantry and cavalry. He assumed joint command with Wallace. Murray had already seized most of the English-held castles in the north of Scotland. Wallace was besieging Dundee Castle when he heard that a fresh English army was marching towards Stirling. He left the siege in the hands of his lieutenant and rode to Stirling with all haste.

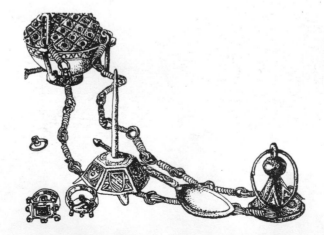

THE BATTLE
OF STIRLING BRIDGE

Though at the time of the War of Independence Stirling Castle consisted mainly of wooden buildings and fencing, it was still regarded as the strongest fortification in Scotland. It held a vital position overlooking the bridge and the fords over the river Forth. Whoever held the castle commanded the main route to the north of Scotland. It had been held by the English since it had capitulated to Edward I the previous year.

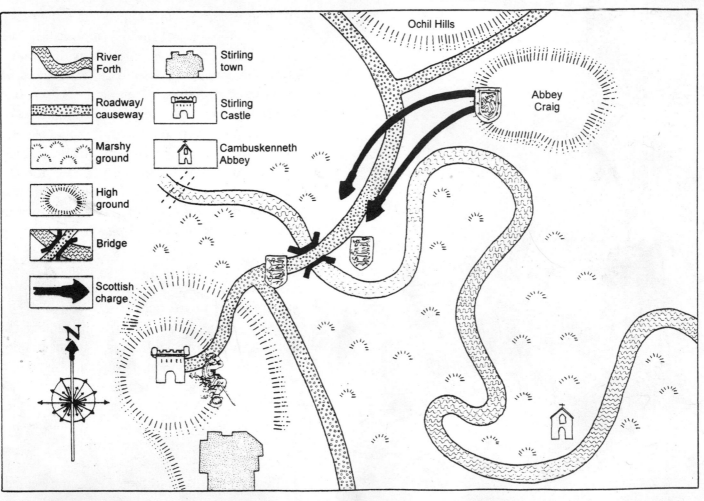

Ochil Hills

Abbey Craig

River Forth

Roadway/causeway

Marshy ground

High ground

Bridge

Scottish charge

Stirling town

Stirling Castle

Cambuskenneth Abbey

N

21

The English army was camped under the rocky crag on the top of which was the castle. The bridge over the Forth was only just wide enough to allow horsemen to cross in pairs. Wallace and Murray drew up their army about 1½ kilometres beyond the bridge on Abbey Craig, an outcrop of the Ochil Hills. Between the bridge and Abbey Craig ran a narrow causeway over marshy ground, on which it would be difficult for the English cavalry to manoeuvre. In the battle the Scots only used foot-soldiers, many of whom were armed with fearsome spears, four metres long.

Early in the morning of 11 September 1297, the vanguard of the English army began to advance, two by two, across the bridge. They were then recalled because their commander, the elderly Earl of Surrey, had overslept and was not yet up. Surrey now sent two friars to invite Wallace to surrender. Wallace sent them back with his answer: 'We are not here to make peace, but to fight for our country's freedom. Let the English come on: we'll meet them beard to beard.'

While the Scots kept to their ranks and waited,

the English began to cross the bridge again. When about half of them were over, Wallace sounded his horn. The whole Scottish army came charging down the hill. Five thousand English cavalry and infantry were now trapped in a loop in the river. Surrey and the rest of his army could only watch in horror at the slaughter of their comrades, many of whom were pushed into the river and drowned.

When Surrey saw that the day was lost, he was so desperate to escape that he rode to Berwick without any stops to feed his horse, which collapsed under him on arrival. He left Stirling Castle in the care of Sir Marmaduke Tweng, who had fought his way back through the Scottish host and over the bridge again. The chief Englishman to die was Hugh Cressingham, Edward I's treasurer and tax-collector in Scotland. After the battle the skin was torn from his body and cut into pieces, which people kept as tokens of Scottish freedom from the hateful rule he represented. He was a fat man, and there was enough skin over for Wallace to have a swordbelt made for himself.

Sir William Wallace

When Stirling Castle surrendered soon after the battle because of lack of provisions, Wallace spared the life of its commander, Sir Marmaduke Tweng, because of his bravery in the field. Wallace also took the towns of Edinburgh, Roxburgh, and Berwick from the English, and burned others south of the river Forth.

Then he and Andrew Murray, both still in their early twenties, took in hand the government of Scotland. In the name of their absent King, John Balliol, they wrote to merchants in German ports encouraging the reopening of trade between the two countries, now that Scotland had been freed

Bishop Fraser of St Andrews, one of the original Guardians, died in 1297. Wallace sent orders from England that his successor as Bishop should be William Lamberton, who was a man equally devoted to the cause of an independent Scotland. Lamberton courageously travelled through seas patrolled by English ships to the Continent, and then overland to Rome, to be consecrated by the Pope.

from the English. They signed themselves 'Commanders of the army of the kingdom of Scotland and the community of that realm'.

Murray died a few weeks later of a wound he had received at the Battle of Stirling Bridge. Wallace, responding to the general feeling that the English should be punished, led an expedition into the northern counties of England.

Since he had no siege weapons with which to subdue castles or take fortified towns, the ordinary people of the countryside and the monks and priests of the monasteries and abbeys suffered most from Wallace's fury. He led his wild Scottish soldiers killing and looting right across the land as far as Cockermouth in the west and Newcastle in the east. When he tried to invade Durham, he was faced with blizzards of snow and ice such as no one had ever seen before in those parts. His men, weighed down with booty, declared that they had had enough; they believed that St Cuthbert, the patron saint of Durham, was protecting his people.

Shortly after Wallace returned from England at the head of his army, he was given two honours by a special council of Scottish lords and

churchmen. The sword of knighthood was buckled round his waist (he was now called Sir William Wallace), and he was elected sole Guardian of Scotland. As Guardian, he had not only to supervise the whole government of the country in the absence of John Balliol, but also to prepare for the next onslaught from Edward I. It was not long coming.

This time Edward was determined that nothing should go wrong, however long it took. He made York, half way between London and Edinburgh, the headquarters of his government. He ordered his army, which included ten thousand heavy armoured cavalry, to meet him at Roxburgh in June 1298. Then, for a month, with food stocks getting low, the English looked for the Scottish army.

At Linlithgow, Edward decided that he had no choice but to retreat to Edinburgh and possibly to abandon the campaign. Just then, he had a report from two Scottish earls who were faithful to the English cause that Wallace and his army were encamped 29 kilometres (18 miles) away, near Falkirk.

It is possible that Wallace was as surprised to find the English advancing against his position as

Edward was to have found his enemy at last. In the months since the Battle of Stirling Bridge, however, Wallace had trained his peasant army in new tactics…

The night before the battle, Edward was so concerned that Wallace might launch a surprise attack that he ordered his men to lie down beside their horses. During the night his own horse trod on him, breaking several of his ribs. The English were already in such a state of alarm that the news of his injury caused panic in their ranks.

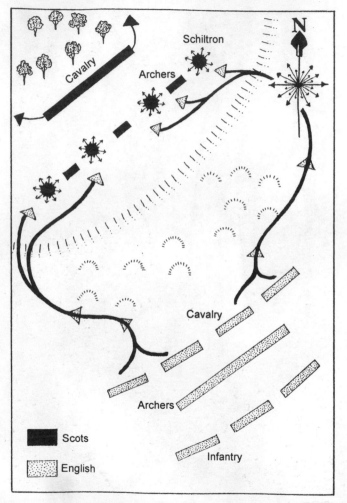

FALKIRK (1298) AND AFTER

Wallace's position was on the slope of a hill, with an area of boggy ground in front, where two burns met. He arranged his spearmen in four huge, circular, human fortresses, called schiltrons. Between the schiltrons he placed his archers, with their short-range bows. Behind them waited the Scottish cavalry, whose job it was to ride down the English bowmen.

The English had not eaten for 24 hours. Edward wanted them to wait for breakfast. He was outvoted by his cavalry commanders, who rode at the Scottish line, swinging to each side when they met the bog. The Scottish horsemen turned and fled. Almost all the Scottish archers died in that first attack, but the schiltrons held firm against several assaults.

Each schiltron contained between 1000 and 2000 men. Those at the outside of the circle knelt on the ground with their spears slanting upwards. More men stood behind, their spears pointing outwards over the shoulders of those in front. The men towards the centre were there to take the place of any who fell. Protecting each schiltron was a row of sharpened stakes, roped together and pointing towards the enemy.

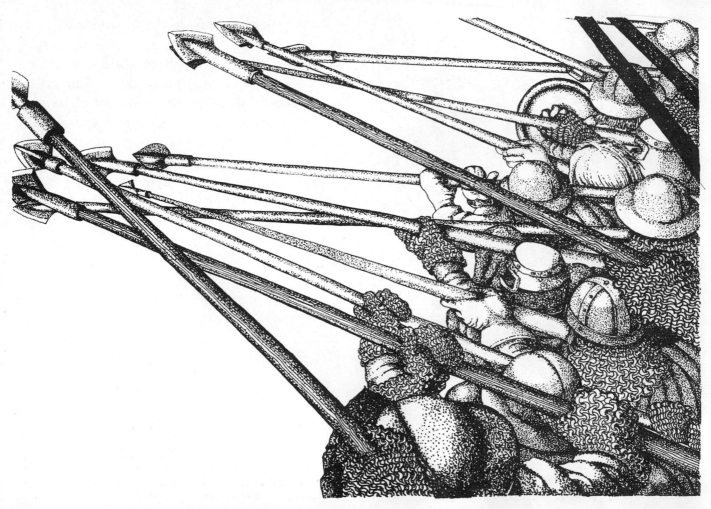

Edward ordered his cavalry to withdraw. Then he unleashed *his* secret weapon, the longbowmen of Sherwood Forest and from Wales, backed up by Continental mercenaries armed with crossbows. From long range, with no Scottish cavalry to oppose them, they picked off man after man in the schiltrons, until it was safe for the cavalry to go in and finish off the rest.

Wallace escaped. As long as he was alive, Edward could not rest. Though Wallace resigned as Guardian and went abroad for a time, Scottish resistance continued.

After campaigning in Galloway in 1300,

To batter Stirling Castle into submission, Edward used vast siege engines, weighted by lead stripped from the roofs of local churches and cathedrals. The defenders held out for three months, and surrendered only because they were starving. Even then, Edward insisted on an extra day's bombardment to try out his new weapon, called the War-Wolf. His Queen and her ladies watched from a window specially built into a house in the town.

Edward, accompanied by Edward of Caernarvon (now Prince of Wales), launched a full-scale invasion in 1303. He had three enormous floating pontoon bridges constructed off the east coast of England at King's Lynn. These were then transported by sea to the Firth of Forth, so that his men could cross over on them direct into Fife. On his way north he met serious opposition only at Brechin Castle, which he subdued with siege engines brought by sea to Montrose. Having progressed as far as Kinloss Abbey in Moray, he returned to Dunfermline for the winter.

In February 1304, representatives of the Scottish nobles formally surrendered to Edward I. He promised in return that under his rule the Scots would have the same rights as during the reign of Alexander III. The nobles did not include Sir John de Soules, the senior of the Guardians who had taken over from Wallace, or Wallace himself.

Edward now had only two pieces of unfinished business. He destroyed Stirling Castle, which its commander claimed had been entrusted to him personally by Sir John. And he continued relentlessly to pursue Wallace.

Wallace was betrayed in Glasgow in August 1305 and taken in chains to London. In Westminster Hall he was accused of a multitude of crimes beginning with the murder of Heselrig, and of being a traitor to Edward I. He was convicted without any defence being heard, and sentenced to a peculiarly horrible death. He was taken straight out, bound to a hurdle, and dragged by horses through the streets. First he was hanged. Then (for his treason) he was cut down while he was still alive and his bowels were torn out and burned. His head was cut off and his trunk was chopped into four pieces, which were sent to Newcastle, Berwick, Perth, and Stirling to be displayed in public. In the eyes of the English Wallace may have been a criminal, but he was not a traitor. For he never put his name to the Ragman Roll.

The Scots had surrendered. Wallace was dead. The War of Independence, however, still went on.

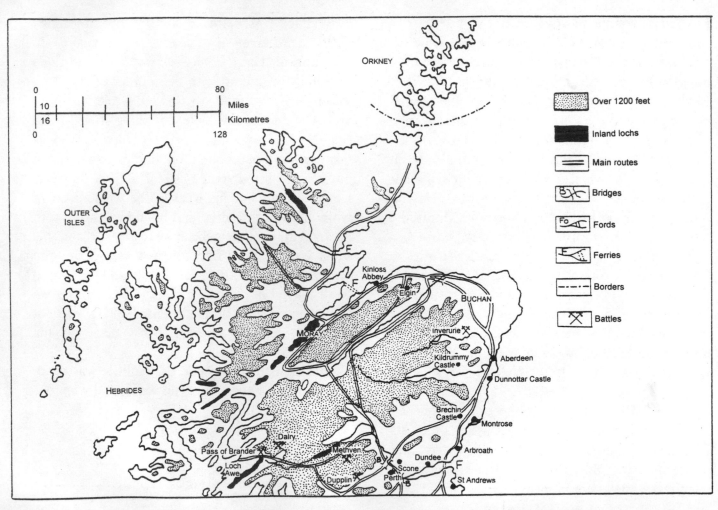

ORKNEY

OUTER
ISLES

0   80
10   Miles
16   Kilometres
0   128

HEBRIDES

F

Kinloss
Abbey
F
Elgin

BUCHAN

MORAY

Inverurie

Kildrummy
Castle

Aberdeen

Dunnottar Castle

Brechin
Castle

Montrose

Dalry

Pass of Brander

Methven

Arbroath

Loch
Awe

B

Dundee

Scone

F

Dupplin

Perth

St Andrews

Over 1200 feet

Inland lochs

Main routes

Bridges

Fords

Ferries

Borders

Battles

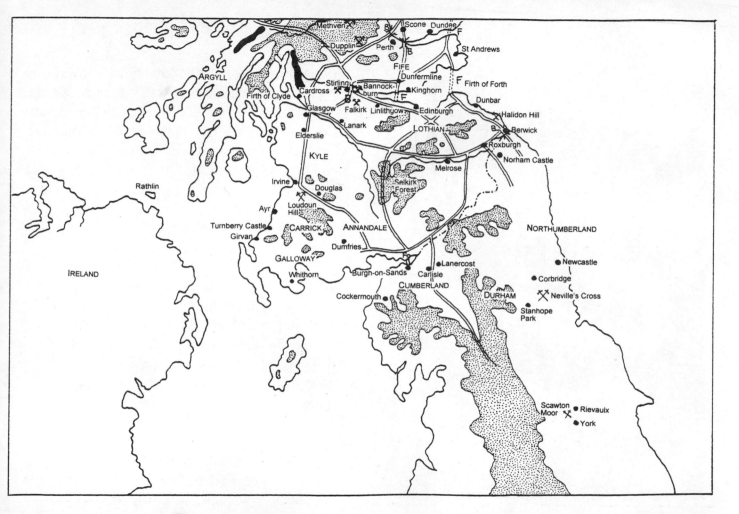

ROBERT THE BRUCE

Robert Bruce, generally known as Robert the Bruce, was probably born at Turnberry Castle, Ayrshire. He was the grandson of Robert Bruce, 'The Competitor'. His father married Marjorie, Countess of Carrick in her own right, as her second husband. Robert the Bruce was the eldest of ten children. He became Earl of Carrick in 1292, when his father resigned the title on being named by *his* father ('The Competitor') successor to the Bruce claim to the throne of Scotland.

During the earlier part of the War of Independence, Robert the Bruce was sometimes on one side, sometimes on the other. We should not be surprised that he and his family signed the Ragman Roll: not to have done so would have meant that they supported John Balliol, to whose throne they felt they had a stronger claim. At the beginning of Wallace's first campaign, however, Bruce led out the men of Carrick in revolt against English rule.

In 1295 Robert the Bruce married Isabel, daughter of the Earl of Mar. She died the next year, having given birth to a daughter, Marjorie.

Robert the Bruce was brought up in a society which valued fighting skills above all. When there were no wars to fight, knights travelled round Europe taking part in tournaments. Bruce was regarded as one of the three bravest and most accomplished knights in the whole of the Christian world. The other two were Henry of Luxembourg, who was later Holy Roman Emperor, and the Englishman Sir Giles d'Argentine, who was to distinguish himself at the Battle of Bannockburn.

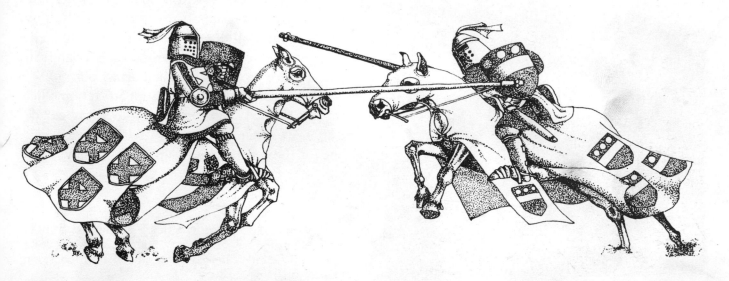

After Wallace resigned as Guardian in 1298, Bruce was appointed joint Guardian with the hot-tempered John Comyn, Lord of Badenoch (known as the Red Comyn). The following year a third Guardian was appointed, Bishop Lamberton. Bruce resigned as Guardian in 1300.

In 1302 Bruce was once more in league with the English. A document survives in which Edward I guarantees freedom and safety to Bruce, his followers, and tenants, and gives him permanent possession of the lands of Carrick. He also undertook to support Bruce in any lawsuit by which John Balliol, or Balliol's son and heir, might try to reclaim the throne of Scotland. In return Bruce promised his good behaviour.

Bruce needed Edward's support for another reason. He had fallen in love with Elizabeth de Burgh, daughter of the Earl of Ulster, who was one of Edward's chief supporters. They were

In 1299 Edward I released John Balliol from house arrest in England into the care of the Pope. From then until his death in 1313, Balliol lived in comfort in various stately houses in France.

married shortly after the terms of the document were agreed.

In 1304, when the Scottish nobles surrendered to Edward I, it was the Red Comyn who had conducted the negotiations. What happened next was not what Edward, or anyone else, expected. After having had secret talks with Bishop Lamberton, Bruce arranged a secret meeting with Comyn in Greyfriars Kirk in Dumfries in February 1306.

Nobody knows what they said to each other. It is most likely that Bruce asked Comyn to support him in a bid for the Scottish throne, and Comyn (whose mother was a sister of John Balliol) hotly refused. Anyway, Bruce stabbed Comyn with his dagger, and his followers dashed in and finished Comyn off with their swords. It was certainly an act of murder. It was also sacrilege, for the killing was done in a church.

The young James Douglas, eldest son of Wallace's ally, William Douglas, was one of Lamberton's household. When he got Bruce's message, the Bishop gave Douglas his own horse and sent him off to join Bruce. Douglas, later known as the Black Douglas or the Good Douglas, became Bruce's closest friend.

KING OF SCOTLAND

Bruce's first act after the murder of Comyn was to seize the castles in and around Dumfries. He also ensured that most of the castles guarding the entrance to the Firth of Clyde were in his hands, so that he could get in supplies and troops from Ireland and the Outer Isles.

Then he made his peace with Robert Wishart, Bishop of Glasgow, in whose diocese Comyn had been murdered. Wishart not only forgave him but provided robes fit for a king to wear and a banner bearing the royal arms of Scotland. In return Bruce promised to uphold the liberties of the Scottish Church and to govern with its assent.

Bruce now sent a message to Bishop Lamberton in Berwick, inviting him to Scone for the coronation. As Robert I, he was made King of Scotland in the Abbey Church of Scone on 25 March 1306. There was no Stone of Destiny on which to be crowned, as Edward I had stolen it. Nor was the Earl of Fife there, who by ancient tradition did the actual crowning of a new King of Scotland; he was only 16 and Edward I had forbidden him to attend.

In his place, the Earl's aunt, Isabella of Fife, Countess of Buchan, crowned Bruce with a gold coronet. Though she was married to the Earl of Buchan, who was an ally of Edward I and a relative of the Red Comyn, she insisted on taking part in the ceremony. She rode to Scone on one of her husband's best war-horses, without his knowledge.

Though Bruce was now King of Scotland, Edward I held all the winning cards! He appointed Aymer de Valence, a brother-in-law of the murdered Comyn, as special commissioner in Scotland, with orders to show no mercy. Bruce was here and there, seizing castles and quelling uprisings. Even Bishop Lamberton and the elderly Bishop Wishart played fighting parts, until they were captured, sent to England, and put in irons in dungeons.

Bruce's attempt to bring de Valence to battle was a disaster. At Methven his troops were surprised and routed. Bruce covered the retreat from the rear, encouraging the survivors and fighting off pursuers. There was another defeat, at Dalry, near Tyndrum, when his party was ambushed by the Macdougalls of Argyll. As Bruce fought off a

swarm of clansmen, one of them, it is said, got close enough to pull the brooch from the King's cloak before being cut down.

Bruce now sent his wife, his daughter Marjorie, his sister Mary, the Countess of Buchan, and other women, to Kildrummy Castle, near Aberdeen, under the protection of his brother Nigel. Then he took a boat to Rathlin, a tiny island off the Irish coast.

No one knows where he went from there. Some say he went to Orkney, then owned by Norway, whose King was the son of Bruce's sister, Isabella Bruce. Others think he took refuge in the Hebrides or in Ireland. He may have visited all three, for sea transport was good in those days.

When he slipped back into Carrick in February 1307, all was gloom and despair. His earldom of Carrick had been confiscated by Edward I, and his former tenants were too frightened to come out in his support. Kildrummy Castle had fallen, and Nigel Bruce had been hanged, drawn, and quartered.

The Queen and Marjorie were in captivity in England. For the brave Countess of Buchan and Mary Bruce, Edward devised a most humiliating punishment. They were shut up in cages jutting out from the castle walls of Roxburgh and Berwick. Food and drink were handed in to them; they were only allowed to retire behind the wall to use the lavatory.

Bruce's brothers Alexander, Dean of Glasgow, and Thomas, whom he had sent ahead with an expeditionary force of 18 ships, had been captured, hanged, and beheaded. All he had were a few loyal companions, forty mounted men provided by a female cousin, Christian of Carrick, and his own strength of character.

It is to the time when he had just returned to Scotland that the legend of Bruce and the spider belongs. As he lay awake one night in a cave, he saw a spider hanging by its thread. Six times it tried to swing itself on to the side wall. When it succeeded at the seventh attempt, Bruce took heart. He would try, try, and try again, until he had recovered his kingdom.

THE RETURN
OF THE KING

Bruce realised that his only hope lay in guerrilla warfare: outwitting and surprising his enemies. Not only the English wanted him dead, but also Scots who still supported the cause of John Balliol or who wanted revenge for the murder of the Red Comyn. There are many stories of Bruce's narrow escapes and of his skill in hand-to-hand fights with men who had been sent to kill him.

In May 1307 he managed to manoeuvre de Valence into fighting a battle in an enclosed space at Loudoun Hill, where his spearmen defeated and routed the English cavalry. Three days later his tiny army scattered a force under the Earl of Gloucester, and chased him back to Ayr.

This was too much for Edward I, who was lying sick and tired at Lanercost Priory, near Carlisle. He got up from his bed, had himself put in a litter at the head of his army, and set out for Scotland. He had only gone a few kilometres when he died, at Burgh-on-Sands. He is supposed to have instructed that his bones should be carried in an urn in front of the army until the Scots were finally defeated. If he did, his son, now Edward II, who hated fighting, took no notice. He buried his father, bones and all, in Westminster Abbey, under a slab inscribed, in Latin, *Scotorum Malleus* (Hammer of the Scots).

Bruce could now concentrate on his Scottish enemies. He was so ill on his way to fight the Earl of Buchan that, when the two forces met at Inverurie, he had to be supported on his horse by a man on each side. At the mere sight of him, the Earl's troops dispersed. Bruce's subsequent treatment of the lands and people of Buchan was so violent that it became remembered as the 'Herschip (ravaging) of Buchan'.

At the Pass of Brander, Bruce beat the Macdougalls at their own game. The track was narrow; on one side was a steep drop down into Loch Awe, and on the other the precipitous slope of Ben Cruachan. The Macdougalls waited in ambush above the track. Unknown to them, Bruce had sent Douglas with a party of bowmen and experienced guerrilla fighters by a roundabout route to a point higher up the mountain.

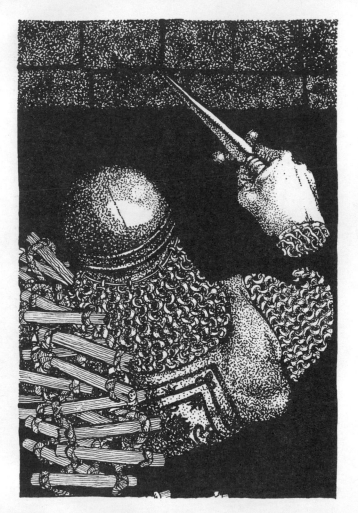

When the Macdougalls began their assault, they were attacked not only from behind, but also by their intended victims, who came at them up the slope. After this victory Bruce felt sufficiently confident to hold his first parliament, at St Andrews in March 1309.

There was still the problem of the English-held fortifications. In 1313, seven years after Bruce had been proclaimed King of Scotland, 21 Scottish towns and castles were still in English hands. He had neither the siege engines to destroy them nor the time or resources to starve them into submission.

Bruce himself commanded the night assault on the town of Perth in January 1313. At the head of his men, he waded through the icy waters of the moat, which came up to his chin, carrying a rope ladder. When the ladders were in position, he was the second man to reach the top of the wall. The town gave in without a fight.

Douglas and his men crawled up to Roxburgh Castle at dead of night and climbed the walls with rope ladders.

While some of the force that Bruce sent against Edinburgh Castle made a noisy diversion, the assault party clambered up the precipice on the other side. They were guided by William Francis, who knew the way from when, as a youth, he had climbed down to visit his girlfriend in the town and then back up again.

In 1313, Edward Bruce, the King's only surviving brother, who had been besieging the strategically vital Stirling Castle without success, made an extraordinary pact with its commander. If no relieving English army came within three miles of Stirling before Midsummer's Day (24 June) 1314, the castle would surrender without a fight. This was a challenge which even the peace-loving Edward II could not honourably ignore. He prepared his army not just to relieve the castle, but to crush the Scots for good. The last thing Bruce wanted, with his small, lightly-armed force, was a full-scale battle. Now he was going to have no choice in the matter…

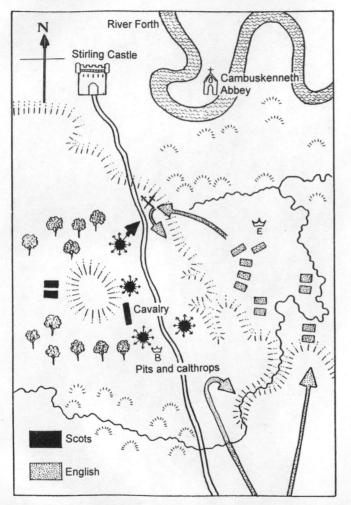

THE BATTLE OF BANNOCKBURN – DAY ONE

On 23 June 1314, with one day to go before the deadline, Edward II led his proud army along the road from Falkirk to Stirling. There were two thousand heavy cavalry and seventeen thousand archers and foot-soldiers. A baggage train of over two hundred wagons carried his army's food, supplies, and pay.

Against this massive force, Bruce had only five hundred light cavalry commanded by Sir Robert Keith, and about five thousand spearmen. The spearmen were in four divisions, roughly according to which part of Scotland they came from. The divisional commanders were the Earl of Moray, James Douglas (who had been knighted the previous evening), Edward Bruce, and the King himself. Learning from the experience of the Battle of Falkirk, Bruce put only about five hundred men into each schiltron, and trained them to advance in step, like huge moving tanks bristling with spears.

Bruce also had in reserve two thousand 'small

folk'. These were mainly farmers, townsmen, craftsmen, and labourers, keen but untrained in war, each man carrying whatever weapons he possessed. Camouflaged pits were dug in the ground across which Bruce guessed the enemy would attack, and calthrops, upturned spikes, spread over it, to deter the English cavalry.

Edward II planned a frontal assault from the south with 1500 cavalry and infantry under the command of the Earl of Gloucester. At the same time Sir Robert Clifford would lead a cavalry force round and behind the Scots, to get between them and Stirling Castle and attack them from the rear.

The battle was almost over before it had begun. Bruce, mounted on a Highland pony to keep his war-horse fresh for the battle, was inspecting his forward divisions when an enemy patrol crossed the burn. An English knight, Sir Henry de Bohun, recognising Bruce by the coronet round his helmet, lowered his lance and charged at him at full gallop. Bruce made his pony skip aside at the last moment and, as de Bohun thundered past, split the Englishman's helmet with one blow of his battle-axe.

A calthrop was made of two pieces of iron twisted and welded together. Whichever way it fell, three of its sharp points formed a tripod for the fourth.

When the battle did start, Gloucester's force met the pits, the calthrops, and the advancing schiltrons, and retreated in confusion. Clifford himself was among the many casualties of the spears of Moray's single mobile schiltron, which lost only one man.

That was the end of fighting for the day. It was about 3pm, and Edward II called a council of war. In spite of advice that the army should stay where it was, Edward insisted on crossing the Bannock Burn with all his knights and soldiers to a point east of the Scottish position. The morale of the English was low, especially as they had now to spend the night without the means of making a camp.

It was Bruce's turn to plan an attack. This was something Edward did not think he would dare to do, such was the difference in numbers between the two armies. Bruce still had problems. During the night the Earl of Atholl, who was meant to be marching to help Bruce, instead, because of a row between the two families, treacherously attacked the Scottish supply base at Cambuskenneth Abbey, killing its commander and his men.

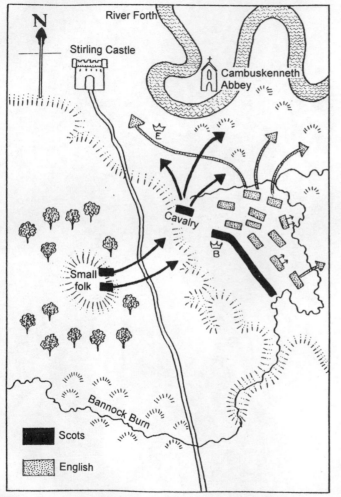

On the map:

N

River Forth

Stirling Castle

Cambuskenneth Abbey

E

Cavalry

B

Small folk

Bannock Burn

■ Scots

▨ English

THE BATTLE OF BANNOCKBURN — DAY TWO

It was a fine, dry morning. The divisions commanded by Edward Bruce, Moray, and Douglas, with the King's spearmen massed behind them, advanced down on to the plain to within a few hundred metres of the English front line. There they knelt down in prayer.

'Ha!' Edward II is reported to have said. 'They kneel for mercy.'

'They are kneeling for mercy, but not from your Majesty,' observed a courtier drily. 'I think they are about to attack!'

The English trumpets sounding the alarm came as such a surprise that the Earl of Gloucester had no time to put on his protective outer coat before leading his cavalry against the advancing Scots. He died, pierced by several spears.

The Scottish spearmen fought, closely locked together, in one line now, advancing as an enormous, elongated, flexible schiltron. Slowly the English were forced back. When they managed to bring a company of archers into action on the

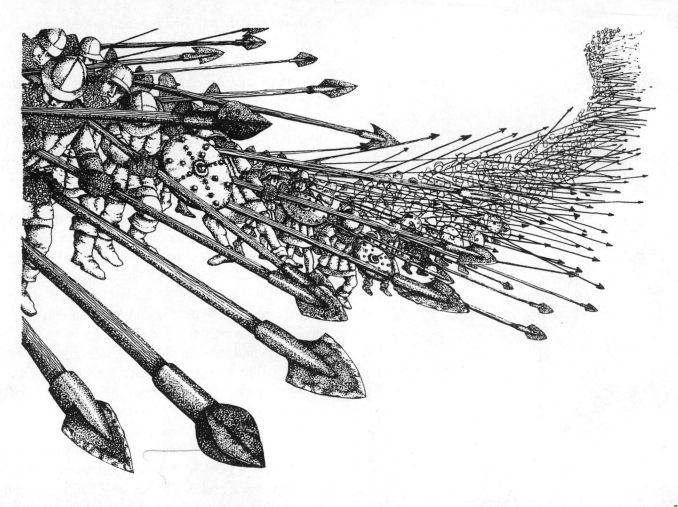

Scottish left flank, Bruce sent in Keith and his light cavalry, who drove them from the battlefield.

Then Bruce brought his own division into the line. This was the turning point of the battle. The fierce Highlanders under Angus Og, Chief of the Macdonalds of the Isles, tore into the English line, causing utter confusion. Edward II, realising the battle was lost, was persuaded by Sir Giles d'Argentine to leave the field.

Having seen Edward II on his way to safety, d'Argentine returned to the battle and charged to his death on the Scottish spears. Edward was advised not to take refuge in Stirling Castle, where he faced certain capture. Instead, pursued all the way, he rode to Dunbar. From there he was taken in a small rowing boat to Berwick.

Meanwhile the 'small folk', waiting in the rear of the battle, either on Bruce's orders or from sheer excitement, raced down the hill in a body. The English, mistaking them for fully-armed reserves, turned and fled. Everywhere they were pursued. Some were drowned in the Forth, some in the evil waters of the Bannock Burn; others were cut down and butchered. The Scots now fell on the English supply waggons, which contained treasure as well as money. It has been estimated that the loot they took would be worth over £50 million today.

It was a complete victory. The English tactics had been appalling, but Bruce had trained his much smaller and less well-equipped army with the greatest skill, and had led it with flair and a deep understanding of warfare. As for Angus Og, Bruce regarded his contribution and that of his clan so highly that ever afterwards the Macdonalds claimed the honour of fighting on the right flank of the front line.

AFTER THE BATTLE

There was now an exchange of prisoners. For the Earl of Hereford, Bruce got back his Queen, his daughter Marjorie, his sister Mary, and Bishop Wishart, who was now blind – Bishop Lamberton had been allowed to return to Scotland in 1309, and the Countess of Buchan had been released from her cage in 1310. Bruce also freed the veteran warrior, Sir Marmaduke Tweng, without ransom, and sent back to their families the bodies of Gloucester and Clifford without asking anything in return.

Yet Edward II, once he got home, flatly refused to recognise Scotland as an independent nation or Bruce as its King. So the Scots took to making lightning raids into the counties of northern England, and the War of Independence went on.

In 1315 Marjorie Bruce married the young Walter, sixth hereditary High Steward (Stewart) of Scotland. The following year, while heavily pregnant, she was thrown from her horse and killed. Surgeons delivered the baby, who became Robert II, the first Stewart King of Scotland.

Bruce was also in trouble with Pope John XXII. The previous Pope, Clement V, had in 1309 belatedly excommunicated not only Bruce for killing Comyn in the church, but also those who had helped him in his rise to power. Pope John refused to recognise Bruce as King of Scotland, addressing letters to him as 'Governor of Scotland'. Bruce sent them back unopened. When Lamberton and three other Scottish bishops ignored a summons to attend the papal court in Rome, they were excommunicated too.

The people of Scotland now took a hand. In 1320, eight earls and 31 barons sent a letter to the Pope, known as the Declaration of Arbroath.

Written in beautiful Latin, it is a dignified but firm request to him to persuade Edward II to leave the Scots in peace and to recognise as their King the man of their choice.

Bruce still had enemies, however, among those who had supported John Balliol and the Red Comyn. At the parliament held at Scone in August 1320 (known as the 'Black Parliament'), 12 people were tried for conspiring against the King. One of them was already dead – his corpse was brought in and set before the judges. Of the rest, three were executed, and two, including the Countess of Strathearn, were sentenced to life imprisonment.

PEACE AT LAST!

In 1322 Edward II's army reached Edinburgh and sacked Holyrood Abbey, but then retreated because there was nothing to eat. Bruce had ordered all cattle to be sent away from Lothian and food stocks to be destroyed. There was just one lame cow left in the whole region.

On their way south the English tried to sack Melrose Abbey, but were scattered by Douglas and his men, who were lurking in the forest. Bruce now advanced far into England. He broke through the English lines at Scawton Moor with a frontal assault up a steep, rocky hillside. He hoped by this to capture Edward II, who was staying at Rievaulx Abbey. Edward just got away in time, leaving his personal possessions and silver. After that, he agreed to a 13-year truce.

The truce lasted only four years. In 1327 Edward was made to abdicate after his Queen,

In 1324, Bruce's Queen, Elizabeth, gave birth to a son, David, who became heir to the throne of Scotland in place of Bruce's grandson, Robert.

Isabella, had seized power. He was later murdered. Bruce, unsure whether Isabella's action was lawful and fed up with English pirate attacks on Scottish ships, chose the coronation day of her 14-year-old son, Edward III, to attack Norham Castle.

That summer Douglas and Moray led a Scottish force deep into England. Edward III, with a fine army, marched north to do battle. He thought he had caught the Scots at Stanhope Park, but he had a bitter disappointment. After making a bold night raid on the English headquarters, the Scottish hobelars (mobile cavalry on small, swift horses) vanished into the rain and mist, leaving Edward in tears.

The English retreated to York, and the Scots devastated Northumberland. The English government, realising that the Scots were not going to be beaten, sent envoys to Bruce, who was in Berwick, to ask for peace.

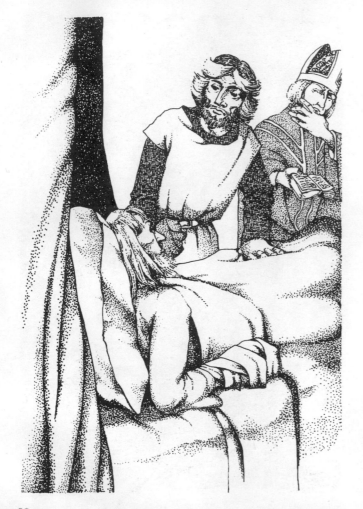

THE DEATH OF THE KING

The peace treaty was finally agreed between the two sides in Edinburgh in March 1328. It was confirmed by the English parliament at Northampton in May. The main points were these: Edward III renounced all claims to rule Scotland and promised to see that the sentences of excommunication on Bruce and his subjects were lifted; a marriage was arranged between Bruce's heir, David, and Edward's sister, Joan of the Tower; the two countries set up a military alliance; Bruce paid Edward £20,000, a very large sum for a poor country.

The royal wedding between David and Joan was in Berwick in 1328: he was four years old and she was just seven. The marriage lasted until her death in 1362. There were no children.

Though the Pope finally cancelled the excommunications in 1328, Bruce was now a very sick man. He insisted, however, on being carried in a litter in slow stages from Girvan to Whithorn. After praying there at the shrine of St Ninian, he was taken back to the royal house he had built at Cardross, where he died on 7 June 1329. His last wish was that his heart should be taken on a crusade to the Holy Land. His body, from which the heart had been cut out, was buried in Dunfermline Abbey. The heart was enclosed in a silver casket and entrusted to Sir James Douglas.

It is said that as Douglas charged into battle against the Saracens, he flung the casket into the enemy and followed behind it. He died fighting. After the battle, the casket was found. The body of the Black Douglas was brought back to Scotland and interred at St Bride's Church, Douglas. The heart of Robert the Bruce lies in Melrose Abbey, though no one knows where it is buried.

The most celebrated Scottish military engagement of the time was conducted by the Countess of Dunbar, known as 'Black Agnes' because of her dark complexion. While her husband was away with the Scottish army in 1338, she defended Dunbar Castle against a large English force equipped with the latest battering rams and siege catapults. After each barrage, she and her maids, dressed in their best clothes, went round the battlements with dusters, wiping the marks that the huge stones and lead balls had made. At the end of five months, during which she often called down rude remarks at the besiegers, the English gave up and went away.

WHAT HAPPENED NEXT?

David II became King when he was five years old. The War of Independence was officially over, but Edward III did not feel bound by the treaty. He supplied troops to Edward Balliol, the son and heir of John Balliol, who landed at Kinghorn and marched unopposed to Dupplin. Having beaten a much larger Scottish force, he entered Perth in triumph, and had himself crowned at Scone. Scotland now had two kings.

After a further Scottish defeat, at Halidon Hill, David was taken away to safety in France. Three famous sons now led the Scottish fight back: John Randolph, son of the Earl of Moray; Marjorie Bruce's son, Robert Stewart, who was now heir to the throne again; and Sir Andrew Murray, the son of Wallace's partner in battle and in government. They were so successful that in 1341 it was felt safe for young David II to return. By this time Edward III had other things on his mind. In 1339 he had begun the Hundred Years War against France.

David's reign was long and inglorious. In 1346 the King of France asked for help under the treaty (later known as the Auld Alliance) which the Guardians had signed fifty years before. While Edward was occupied in France, David led his army into England, and was defeated and captured at Neville's Cross. He spent the next 11 years as a closely-guarded prisoner in London.

He returned to Scotland after the first instalment of a large ransom had been paid. By this time Robert Stewart, as Regent of Scotland, had rid the country of the English, and Edward Balliol had given up his crown in return for a comfortable pension. When David died, still childless, in 1371, Robert, now 55, became the first Stewart King of Scotland.

INDEX